Theatre503 and FallOut Theatre
present

The World Premiere

Meat
Blood, Skin and Bone

by Jimmy Osborne
Developed with David Aula for FallOut Theatre

Playdead Press

Published by Playdead Press 2012

© Jimmy Osborne 2012

Jimmy Osborne has asserted his rights under the Copyright, Design and Patents Act, 1988, to be identified as the author of this work.

A CIP catalogue record for this book is available from the British Library.

ISBN 978-0-9572859-1-0

Playdead Press
www.playdeadpress.com

Meat by Jimmy Osborne
First performance at Theatre503, Battersea, 5 June 2012

Cast in alphabetical order

Joy	**Tracy Brabin**
Vincent	**Graham Turner**
Rob/Sandra	**Ian Weichardt**
Carla	**Charlotte Whitaker**

The performance lasts approximately 75 minutes.
There will be no interval.

Director	**David Aula**
Designer	**James Cotterill**
Lighting Designer	**Elliot Griggs**
Sound Designer	**Edward Lewis**
Fight Director	**Alison De Burgh**
Casting Director	**Annie Rowe**
Production Manager	**Tom Richardson**
Stage Managers	**Peta Dyce and Jude Malcomson**
Assistant Director	**Niall Wilson**
Design Assistant	**Lucie Wright**
Producers	**Theatre503; James Baggaley and Ollie Jordan**

Jimmy Osborne Playwright

Jimmy Osborne is a graduate of the Young Writers Programme at the Royal Court Theatre where he had rehearsed readings of two of his plays, *Ripples* and *Windows*. Jimmy was a member of the Crossing the Borders international writing project and a writer in residence at Chelsea and Westminster Hospital, where he contributed to the *Under the Skin* drama project. His Short play, *This is Jack, Leave a Message, Alright?* recently won a national BBC Writersroom competition and has been performed at the Etcetera Theatre, London. His most recent short play, *Transmission*, was performed as part of *Little Pieces of Love* at the Southwark Playhouse in February 2012. Twitter: @OsborneJimmy

David Aula Director

David is the Artistic Director of FallOut Theatre.
Theatre as director: *Personal Enemy* by John Osborne (Theater 59E59 New York, White Bear Theatre London), *Mummies and Daddies* by Torben Betts (White Bear), *Something/Nothing* by Rory Mullarkey (Abbey Mills), *Hamlet* (European Tour), Anton Chekov's *Three Sisters* trans. Rory Mullarkey (ADC).
David is currently working on a stage adaption of Ian McEwan's *The Cement Garden* with Jimmy Osborne.

Tracy Brabin Joy

Theatre: *Long Road* (Curve), *Confusions* (Number One tour), *Stiff Options* (Number One tour), *Trafford Tanzi* (Bristol Old Vic), *Road* (Bolton Octagon), *Tom Jones, Strictly Ballroom* (Swan Theatre, Worcester)
Television: *Coronation Street* (3 years), *Outside Edge* (3 series), *A Bit Of A Do* (2 series), *Ghost Hunter* (3 series), *Strictly Confidential* (2 series), *Eastenders, Bodies, Nice Guy Eddie, Silent Witness, Where The Heart Is, Heartbeat, Holby, Casualty, The Good Samaritan, The Bill, Rosemary And Thyme,*

Midsummer Murders, Doctors, Sunburn, Hale And Pace,Peak Practise, El C.I.D.

Film: *Piercing Brightness* (Dir Shezad Dawood), *Love + Hate* (dir: Dominic Savage), *A Palace Divided* (ABC TV), *Riff Raff* (Dir: Ken Loach). For two years she also played Sarah in *Sainsbury's* TV advertising campaign.

Tracy is also a writer and her writing credits include: *Crossroads, Tracy Beaker, Family Affairs, Heartbeat, Hollyoaks* and *Shameless*. She has two features in development with Phil Davis and Minkie Spiro attached to direct. She has just finished her first teen novel *Paradise.*

James Cotterill Designer

Recent designs include; *Good*; *A View from the Bridge*; *Powder Monkey*; *Mojo Mickybo* (Royal Exchange Theatre), *Straight*; *The Pride*; *That Face* (Crucible Studio), *The Seven Year Itch* (Salisbury Playhouse), *Macbeth*; *The Demolition Man* (Bolton Octagon), *Accolade* (Finborough Theatre), *The Flint Street Nativity*; *The Elves And The Shoemaker* (Hull Truck), *The Wages of Thin* (Old Red Lion) (Off West End.Com Nomination for Best Set), *Estate Walls* (Oval House). In 2005 he was a winner of the Linbury Prize for Stage Design for *Not The End Of The World* at Bristol Old Vic. In 2009 his installation *Smash Here* was chosen by Time Out to be part of the Deloitte Ignite festival at the Royal Opera House. Other designs include: *The Eleventh Capital*; *Gone Too Far!* (Royal Court Upstairs), *A Little Neck* (Goat & Monkey at Hampton Court Palace), *The Musician* (OMAC, Belfast), *Lough/Rain* (Theatre Royal, York), *So Close to Home* (Arcola Theatre & Brighton Festival), *Spies* (Theatre Alibi, Oxford Playhouse & Tour), *The Pleasure Principle* (Tristan Bates), *Romeo & Juliet* (BAC), *Big Sale* (Protein Dance/The Place & UK Tour), *Fair* (Trafalgar Studio 2), *Silverland*; *15 Minutes* (Arcola Theatre), *Widows*; *The Fool* (Vanbrugh Theatre, RADA).

Elliot Griggs Lighting Designer

Trained at the Royal Academy of Dramatic Art.

Theatre: *Belleville Rendez-Vous* (Greenwich Theatre), *Lagan* (Oval House Theatre), *Crush, Perchance to Dream, Portraits, And I and Silence, Northern Star* (Finborough Theatre), *Folk Contraption* (Southbank Centre), *The Custard Boys* (Tabard Theatre), *Dealing With Clair, One Minute, dirty butterfly, Nocturnal, Our Town* (Royal Academy of Dramatic Art), *Much Ado About Nothing* (Belgrade Theatre, Coventry), *The Mercy Seat* (RSC CAPITAL Centre), *The Lady's Not For Burning, West Side Story, 'Tis Pity She's a Whore, By The Bog of Cats, Elephant's Graveyard* (Warwick Arts Centre), *Dido and Aeneas* (St. Paul's Church and Touring)

Awards: Francis Reid Award, Association of Lighting Designers, 2011, ShowLight Award, for Elephant's Graveyard, National Student Drama Festival, 2009

Edward Lewis Sound Designer

Edward studied Music at Oxford University and subsequently trained as a composer and sound designer at the Bournemouth Media School. He works in theatre, film, television and radio. He has recently been nominated for several Off West End Theatre Awards, and films he has recently worked on have won several awards at the LA International Film Festival and Filmstock International Film Festival.

Recent theatre includes: *Gravity* (Birmingham Rep Theatre), *On The Rocks, Amongst Friends and Darker Shores* (Hampstead Theatre), *Slowly, Hurts Given and Received and Apple Pie* (Riverside Studios), Measure For Measure (Cardiff Sherman), *Emo* (Bristol Old Vic and Young Vic), *Once Upon A Time in Wigan and 65 Miles* (Paines Plough / Hull Truck Theatre), *Krapp's Last Tape and Spoonface Steinberg* (Hull Truck), *The Shallow End* (Southwark Playhouse), *I Am Falling* (Sadler's Wells & The Gate, Notting Hill), *The Beloved* (The Bush), *The Stronger, The Pariah* (The Arcola), *Madness*

In Valencia (Trafalgar Studios), *The Madness Of George III,
Kalagora and Macbeth* (National Tours), *Knives In Hens*
(Battersea Arts Centre), *Personal Enemy* (White Bear & New
York*)*, *Accolade, Beating Heart Cadaver* and *Mirror Teeth*
(Finborough Theatre).

Annie Rowe Casting Director

Annie trained as an actress at the NYT and RADA before
beginning a career in casting in 2007. In 2011 she gained
Probationary Membership of the Casting Directors' Guild of
Great Britain.

Theatre For Theatre503 includes: *Man In The Middle, The
Swallowing Dark* (with Liverpool Playhouse), *Sold, The Biting
Point, The Charming Man, Breed, Wild Horses, Porn – The
Musical, The Tin Horizon.*

Other theatre includes: *Skanky* (Arcola) *Family, the workshop*
(Sheffield Crucible) *Bee Detective* (Tin Bath Theatre Co) *The
Art Of Concealment* (Jermyn Street) *Fit and Proper People*
(Soho Theatre/ RSC) *Mr Happiness, The Water Engine* (Old
Vic Tunnels), *Love On the Dole* (Finborough), *Alice Through
The Looking Glass, Around The World in 80 Days* (The Egg at
Theatre Royal Bath), *Public Property* (Trafalgar Studios)
Short film includes: *The Heart Of Dicken Partridge, Sound
Asleep, Waiting For Dawn, By Hook, Trailing Dirt, Modo and
Mahu.* Many corporate films, promos, virals and advertising
campaigns for BDA Creative.

Graham Turner Vincent

Theatre includes *King Lear* (West Yorkshire Playhouse) *Alice*
(Sheffield Crucible), *A Midsummer Night's Dream* (Zurich
Ballet), *When We Are Married* (Liverpool Everyman and West
Yorkshire Playhouse), *The Dresser* (Watford Palace), *Arsonist*
and *Rhinoceros* (Royal Court), *Comfort Me With Apples*
(Hampstead Theatre & Tour), *Enemies* (Almeida), *Girl in the
Goldfish Bowl* (Sheffield Crucible), *Talking Heads (*York Theatre

Royal), *Death of a Salesman* (Compass Theatre), *The Norman Conquests* (Clwyd Theatr Cymru), *Hobson's Choice* (Lyric) and seasons at Chichester and the RSC.

Television work includes *Waking the Dead* , *Luther, Casualty, Criminal Justice, Holby City, Blair, Where The Heart Is, Midsomer Murders, Murder In Mind, Bad Girls, MerseyBeat, Dinnerladies, Wide Eyed and Legless, The Battle for The Bible, The Bill* and *Doctors*.

Film work includes *Little Voice, The Duel, Friends and Enemies* and *Fast Food*.

Ian Weichardt Rob/Sandra

Ian trained at the Birmingham School of Acting, where he graduated with a 1st class BA Honours degree.

Television: *DCI Banks* (Left Bank Pictures), *Candy Cabs* (Splash Media), *Coronation Street* (Granada), *Watch Over Me* (Iron Shoes Production), *Miss Marple* (Granada).

Film: *Passengers* (Ratio:Film), *Where's Your Line?* (Rattling Stick), *Physics* (Quiddity Films).

This is Ian's professional theatre debut.

Charlotte Whitaker Carla

Trained at Arts Ed, School of Acting

Theatre: *Smoking in the Boys' Room* (Theatre503), *The Meeting* (Pleasance Islington/Edinburgh), *GRAFT* (Pleasance Islington), *Sonnet Walk* (Shakespeare's Globe Theatre), *The Merchant of Venice* (The Royal Opera House, Covent Garden)

Film: *Welcome to Neverland*

Niall Wilson Assistant Director

Theatre: *Othello* (Lion and Unicorn Theatre), *Twelfth Night* (Lion and Unicorn), *Festen* (ADC Theatre), *All My Sons* (ADC Theatre), *Rum and Vodka* (Corpus Playroom) and *Doubt* (Corpus Playroom). Niall is a graduate of the Royal Court Young Writer's Programme."

Theatre503

Theatre503 is the home of fearless, irreverent, brave and provocative new plays. Working with the most important artists of today and discovering the foremost voices of tomorrow, we push at the boundaries of what theatre can be and pose the unanswerable questions of our time. Theatre503 has proudly premiered over 50 of the most exciting writers of our generation, including Dennis Kelly, Phil Porter, Duncan Macmillan, Rachael Wagstaff, Ali Taylor, Rex Obano and Lou Ramsden. In November 2006 Tim Roseman and Paul Robinson were appointed Artistic Directors; their vision is to develop 503 as a crucible where writers, directors, actors and designers think better and bolder than they would expect. We seek out, nurture and promote work of uncommon and exceptional promise from artists both fresh off the boat and weathered with success. Since 2007 we have striven to become the most important theatre in the UK for first-time playwrights, providing that vital launch pad into public performance. The Mountaintop by Katori Hall started life at Theatre503 before transferring to the West End where it won the Olivier Award for Best New Play, the only time ever a theatre our size has been recognised this way. It opened in October 2011 on Broadway starring Samuel L. Jackson and Angela Bassett.

Artistic Directors | **Tim Roseman** and **Paul Robinson**
General Manager | **Jeremy Woodhouse**
Producer | **Flavia Fraser-Cannon**
Associate Director | **Lisa Cagnacci**
Literary Manager | **Steve Harper**
Literary Coordinator | **Graeme Thompson**
Resident Assistant Producers | **Euan Borland** and **Tara Finney**
Intern | **Valeria Carboni**

FallOut Theatre

FallOut Theatre is committed to the drama of aftermath, the beauty of chance, and the overwhelming energy of conflict.

Formed in 2007, FallOut Theatre was originally a collaboration between David Aula and Dr Abigail Rokison. They met at the University of Cambridge where they were thrown together by a production of *4:48 Psychosis* by Sarah Kane, which David directed. Abigail acted in the first two FallOut productions, *After the End* and *The Cement Garden* and directed its third, *The Pillowman* by Martin McDonagh - in which David played Tupolski. The company moved to London in 2009, Abigail remains in her position as Director of Studies for English and Drama in the Faculty of Education. She continues to support and tutor the work of young actors and directors and complements her acclaimed academic work (Shakespearean Verse Speaking: Text and Theatre Practice, Cambridge University Press) by continuing to produce high quality theatre.

In 2010, FallOut Theatre produced the first full production of Torben Betts' brutal critique of consumerist culture, *Mummies and Daddies*, as well as *Personal Enemy* by John Osborne and Antony Creighton – lost for over half a century by the Lord Chamberlain's office who had censored its contents of all reference to homosexuality. *Personal Enemy* opened in London in June 2010, before transferring to the Brits Off Broadway Festival in New York, in November of the same year.

FallOut's next project is an update of its adaptation of Ian McEwan's *The Cement Garden* by David Aula and Jimmy Osborne, the new text of which had a rehearsed reading at the National Theatre Studio in December 2011.

Artistic Director | **David Aula**
Writer-in-Residence | **Jimmy Osborne**
Producers | **Ollie Jordan** and **James Baggaley**
Associate Artists | **Jack Monaghan, Rebecca Pitt** and **Patrick Warner**

You can support FallOut's work by becoming a Friend of FallOut Theatre by donating via our website, or contact us for more information.

FallOut Theatre is grateful for the support of its Friends: **Caitlin Birley, Adrian Cook, Martin and Claire Daunton, Lucy Flett, Ian Gerrard, Ruth and Dion Harrison, Joan Osborne, Andrew Perkins, Toby Sawyer, Damian Shepherd, David and Anne Talbot, Andrew Voysey, Neil Warner**

Meat was generously supported by the Mercers Foundation.

FallOut Theatre would also like to thank:
David Birley and Sally Carr, Valerie Burgess, Francesca Clark, Sophia Galitzine, Clare Jordan, Neil McPherson.

Meat was rehearsed at St Francis de Sales Church Hall, Stockwell, London.
For hire enquiries, contact Val Burgess:
valstfrancis@gmail.com

FallOut Theatre
www.fallouttheatre.com | contactus@fallouttheatre.com
Registered Charity no. 1124476

For Jem.

Properly and Everything.

Author's Thanks
David Aula and FallOut Theatre for collaboration
and good times.
Paul Robinson, Tim Roseman, Steve Harper and
all at Theatre503 for faith, love and support.
Simon Burt, Laura Jessop, Aoife Mannix, Rory
Mullarkey, Dan O'Carroll, Julie Press and Simon
Stephens for advice, thoughts and provocation

Meat

by
Jimmy Osborne

Characters

Vincent – mid 40's, slaughterman.

Joy – 40, married to Vincent.

Carla – 17, their daughter.

Rob – 17, a local lad.

Sandra – mid 40's, Rob's Mother

Sandra is doubled by the actor playing Rob.

Note on the dialogue

A '/' highlights where one characters speech overlaps with another's.

Blood

The deafening sound of the abattoir at work — cattle being brought in, machinery, people working.
The sounds fade.
*Enter **VINCENT**, wearing a white slaughterman's apron stained with old blood.*

VINCENT   You have to cut the carotid artery in the neck. Clean and fast. Let the blood flow out. And you've got to do it with the noise of the animals dying. The bolt gun. The machines playing. The taste of zinc in the air. You put all that out of your mind. Do a good job. You keep up with the line.

You have to be handy with the steel. The animal gets bolted. Strung up. Comes to you in seconds. In mid-air. Hanging from a chain. You see the sweet spot on the neck you need to stick. You should be able to stick it in one go. You have to cut the carotid artery. Clean and fast. Keep your knife sharp. You pass the animal on. Down the line. To men and women. To machines. Quickly disassembled. Doesn't take long. Least. As long as the job's done right. These young lads we have now. Supposed to bolt them properly. Right in the brain. Knock it out. But they've no idea. I've seen them. Seen them have to bolt a cow three times. Four times. Thought the cow was going to have to take matters into it's own hands. Do the job itself. Death here is supposed to be quick. We've a quota to get through. And the quota keeps going up. But you push all that down. You can't think. You think too much. You don't keep up with the line. You don't keep up with the line. It backs up. It backs up. You don't hit the quota. You don't hit the quota. They hit your pay. You keep up with the line. You don't think. You just act. Smoothly and accurately. You don't pause. You don't wonder what you'll do. You just act.

Enter JOY.

JOY	It's not right what they're doing.
VINCENT	You don't think. You just act.
JOY	You should tell them, Vincent
VINCENT	You don't think.
JOY	tell them it's not right, they're taking
VINCENT	There's work needs finishing, Joy.
JOY	advantage, that's what they're doing, and it's not, I'm thinking of you, you're getting home later and later, nearly eleven tonight, what time is that for
VINCENT	When it's finished.
JOY	for someone to be working. That's beyond the call of duty, Vincent, above and beyond
VINCENT	It'll be finished.
JOY	The call of duty. It's too cold to be working this late too
VINCENT	Come rain or shine.
JOY	cold by half. Did you wear your coat, your blue coat, did you wear it?
VINCENT	Yes.

JOY	With the sheepskin lining? It's getting later and later, you should come home earlier.
VINCENT	I'll thank you not to tell me how to do my job, Joy.
JOY	Th...that's not what I...I wasn't saying.
VINCENT	I'll decide what needs doing when.
JOY	You will, I know you will, that's not, because I wasn't, Vincent, I wasn't. Your job is your job.

BEAT.

JOY	I wouldn't interfere, you know that.
VINCENT	Quota's been put up.
JOY	But they work
VINCENT	I make sure the job's done properly.
JOY	you far too hard.
VINCENT	You appreciate that.
JOY	You know I do...but
VINCENT	There can be no buts. No buts Joy. You decide to do something then you do it. You do not 'but' about it.
JOY	But
VINCENT	You should understand that.

JOY   Yes.

VINCENT   Things must be done properly.

JOY   I know, Vincent, I know.

PAUSE.

VINCENT   I had this sheep today.

JOY   Please don't talk about that place

VINCENT   Sheep stink.

JOY   not again, you know it makes

VINCENT   I walk the line. Before each shift.

JOY   it makes me feel queasy.

VINCENT   Have to know everything is as it should be.
                 This sheep is kicking.

JOY   Please, Vincent

VINCENT   It's been stunned. Been stuck. Been
                 skinned by the machines.

JOY   I hate it.

VINCENT   They do one quick pull. Like a magician
                 whipping off a tablecloth.

JOY   We've always had an agreement

VINCENT   The sheep is still kicking.

JOY   you don't bring it home.

VINCENT   There are always twitchers. Messages still
                 running round the body. Nerves.

JOY	You've been like this all week, all
VINCENT	I can tell. When it's nerves. Or when it's still alive.
JOY	blood and guts
VINCENT	These lads. They're standing there. Laughing at the puppet show.
JOY	and I really don't like it.
VINCENT	I read the spasms of the body. Dodge the thrashing legs.
JOY	Puts me off my dinner.
VINCENT	Get in close. See the cut. Barely broken the skin.
JOY	There's left over pork chops in the fridge
VINCENT	It's alive.
JOY	if you like
VINCENT	Can't stop it dying. But it'll suffer.
JOY	likely to be a little dry now.
VINCENT	I stick it again. Put it out of its misery. Damn near took its head off.
JOY	I could heat them up for you.
VINCENT	Job has to be done properly.
JOY	Carla should be back by now.
VINCENT	Has to.

JOY	The last bus should be here.
VINCENT	Go to bed. I'll wait for her.
JOY	I can't.
VINCENT	I said I'll wait.
JOY	How can I sleep with Carla up town and that boy's killer out there? I asked her not to go out. It's too soon.
VINCENT	She can take care of herself.
JOY	I can't sleep, no one round here sleeps, they're all trembling under their duvets.
VINCENT	You don't need to worry.
JOY	The killer could be outside now, the vermin, outside the back door, prowling around
VINCENT	You're safe.
JOY	on the decking.
VINCENT	You're safe.
JOY	How do you know, I hear all sorts of noises in the house
VINCENT	Nobody would harm you.
JOY	when you're not here? Noises, like someone trying the door or forcing the
VINCENT	/ Wind.

JOY	window / that's how they get in you know. You can't be sure that no one
VINCENT	No one would. Everyone round here knows me. Knows I don't stand for any bother.
JOY	If it's not a murderer it'll be the rats, they're still up in the loft, I can hear them scuttering about, keeping me awake at night, you should
VINCENT	I'll deal with it.
JOY	get some poison and the find the nest, it's been a week.
VINCENT	I'm sorting it.
JOY	They'll be in the rest of the house before we know it.
VINCENT	Go to bed, Joy.
JOY	That poor, poor boy, I can't stop thinking about him.
VINCENT	Bit late for that now.
JOY	A young boy killed like that, it's horrible, horrible...horrible isn't the right word.
VINCENT	What is?
JOY	*(THINKS)* Heartbreaking is what it is, one hundred percent

VINCENT	He wasn't a boy.
JOY	heartbreaking...what?
VINCENT	He was not a boy.
JOY	Seventeen years old.
VINCENT	That is not a boy.
JOY	It's a boy to me, he was the same age as our
VINCENT	He can get married. Drive a car. Work. There's lads at the abattoir younger.
JOY	Don't bring up that place
VINCENT	He was not a boy.
JOY	not again, it makes me feel...it's heartbreaking.
VINCENT	Could've deserved it.
JOY	Vincent! You cannot say that, you cannot say
VINCENT	No one ever comes out on the TV and say, "I'm glad the useless bastard's dead. Good riddance."
JOY	Language, please.
VINCENT	Sounds like the best thing all round.
JOY	Promise me you will not say that to anyone, promise me. It's only been a week.

VINCENT	One less scumbag.
JOY	People, the people will
VINCENT	I've seen the people on the TV. Shocked.
JOY	The community is shocked.
VINCENT	So shocked they have to get on the TV and tell everyone how shocked they are.
JOY	Well it is.
VINCENT	Shocking?
JOY	Yes.
VINCENT	Sheep. One says it and they all start bleating the same thing.
JOY	Everyone is very
VINCENT	Baa.
JOY	upset
VINCENT	Baa!
JOY	they're all very upset.
VINCENT	That lad wasn't the type to spend his time writing poetry and doing charity work.
JOY	Is this about the shop?
VINCENT	Spent his time with his mates. Intimidating old ladies outside the shop.
JOY	I knew you'd bring up the shop.
VINCENT	With every right.

JOY	It was one time.
VINCENT	Talking to me like that.
JOY	Mr Patel's still cross about that
VINCENT	Patel...
JOY	He doesn't like scenes outside his shop.
VINCENT	It was Patel's fault I was down there in the first place. Who does he think he is? Not giving you your holiday when you ask.
JOY	His wife
VINCENT	Patel-
JOY	had been hit by a car.
VINCENT	Don't interrupt.

*Enter **ROB**, music playing on his phone.*

VINCENT	Patel always needs things spelling out.
JOY	You should have walked on by.
VINCENT	That lad and his mates. Standing outside the shop. Like they own the place.
JOY	I always ignored them.
VINCENT	He needed bringing down a peg or two. I had my eye on him.

*__ROB__ looks round, notices **VINCENT**, stares for a moment then turns back to his phone.*

BEAT.

*ROB turns back to **VINCENT**.*

ROB　　　　　What you looking at? I said, what are you looking at?

VINCENT　　　Dunno, but it's looking back. Turn that racket off.

ROB　　　　　Music too loud for you? Sorry, sorry I'm really sorry, yeah? Properly and everything. 'Ere, let me turn it off for you.

ROB turns the music up.

ROB　　　　　That better?

*ROB turns away from **VINCENT**.*

VINCENT thinks about leaving, stays.

VINCENT　　　Said turn it off.

ROB　　　　　You fancy me, that it?

VINCENT　　　I asked you nicely, lad.

ROB　　　　　You wanna watch yourself, you'll be locked up staring at lads like that, people'll think you're a perv, you wanna watch yourself. I don't like perv's looking at me.

VINCENT　　　Little boy's shouldn't have big mouths.

ROB　　　　　Funny, really very funny. A right proper comedian, aren't you?

ROB laughs sarcastically, stops suddenly.

ROB	I'm being polite aren't I? No swearing, minding my p's and q's, and you go an insult me. That's not nice, really not nice at all. I should be compensated. Twenty quid.
VINCENT	Give over, you streak of piss.
ROB	Twenty quid, now, see, I told the lads I'd get us some coin.
VINCENT	You want money. Get a job.
ROB	Twenty quid.
VINCENT	Or what?
ROB	Or...I know you. Yeah, I know you, you're the butcher.
VINCENT	I'm a slaughterman.
ROB	Chopping up animals. I bet that's a laugh. Covered in blood. Killing stuff. Do you ever, you know, mess about with them animals, you know, I bet you do, make 'em squeal?

BEAT

I stamped on a baby sparrow once.

*BEAT – **ROB** stamps his foot, makes **VINCENT** jump.*

ROB   You need to calm down mate, there's six of
               us.

VINCENT   Need your boyfriends to hold your hand?

PAUSE – it could go either way.

ROB   I like you, Mr Butcher, so we'll leave it this
               time.

ROB turns back to his mates.

VINCENT heads to the shop.

ROB   That your daughter I see in the shop now
               and then?

VINCENT   You what?

ROB   The gobby cow.

VINCENT   Don't you be talking about Our Carla.

ROB   Nice arse on it.

VINCENT   You little…

ROB   Me and the lads'd give her a go.

VINCENT   You even look at her funny

ROB   One at a time

VINCENT   or all together and I'll batter you.

ROB   She'd like that.

VINCENT grabs ROB.

VINCENT   Shut your mouth!

ROB isn't scared. Smiles.

ROB	Twenty quid. There's six of us.
VINCENT	You lot get back.
ROB	Give me your fucking wallet now!

VINCENT lets ROB go.

VINCENT	Don't come any closer. Any of you, I'm warning
ROB	The wallet!
VINCENT	Any closer and
JOY	It's a good job I came out when I did…
VINCENT	You had no right butting in Joy. No right.
JOY	I had to do something, it was getting
VINCENT	Made me look
ROB	Hiding behind her fat arse.
JOY	I had visions of I don't know what happening.
VINCENT	Little runt.

ROB makes chicken noises.

Exit ROB.

JOY	There's no shame in being scared
VINCENT	Who was scared?
JOY	Your face was bright ketchup.

VINCENT	His sort don't worry me.
JOY	Now look at the poor boy
VINCENT	Needed putting in his place.
JOY	his picture all over the papers, just awful.
VINCENT	No surprise what happened. With the mouth on him.
JOY	He didn't deserve that.
VINCENT	A matter of opinion.
JOY	You haven't been saying
VINCENT	They don't remember.
JOY	these things
VINCENT	The people.
JOY	to people have you? Say you haven't?
VINCENT	People don't remember that Robert now.
JOY	Vincent…?
VINCENT	How he was always in trouble with the police. No. He's been transformed by death into an angel. Worshipped. People leave flowers and cards at his altar. Where they found him in the gutter.
JOY	You mustn't, you mustn't say these things
VINCENT	I'll say what I like.
JOY	not to anyone.

VINCENT	To who I like.
JOY	Not to anyone, please Vincent, please don't say anything.
VINCENT	Someone should talk sense.
JOY	For me, Vincent, do it
VINCENT	This tragedy's getting out of hand.
JOY	for me. If you say anything they'll throw me off the Funeral Committee – I'm on sandwiches.
VINCENT	Sandwiches?
JOY	For the do after.
VINCENT	It's called a wake.
JOY	Doreen Phillips has been eyeing up my spot. She's looking for any excuse to get me bumped off, You know what she's like, and if you go around
VINCENT	I won't talk to that flock of harpies.
JOY	saying these things...you won't say anything?
VINCENT	What did I just say, woman?
JOY	Thank you, thank you Vincent, you don't know how much...you see, there's a chance, just a chance mind, that if I play

	my cards right, I might be one of the few who walk with Sandra.
VINCENT	Sandra?
JOY	His Mum.
VINCENT	The lad's mother?
JOY	I may get to walk with her at the funeral.
VINCENT	What?
JOY	Maggie Sharp's husband, Roy, has to have his gall bladder out the day of the funeral – too much of the drink they say. Maggie's trying to do both, she was first round there with flowers when everyone heard, but I can't see how she can, there's no way. The funeral's at twelve and Roy's operation is one thirty. She can't make both and if she can't...
VINCENT	We're not going to the funeral.
JOY	Everyone's going, they say they'll be over two hundred.
VINCENT	I'm not putting on a shirt and tie. For him.
JOY	Vincent.
VINCENT	No.

JOY	Please, I might get to walk with...I don't want to let her down.
VINCENT	You barely know the woman.
JOY	We've got
VINCENT	Make your sandwiches.
JOY	to go. People will wonder.
VINCENT	Make your sandwiches if you like. But we're not going.
JOY	I've seen a dress. It's been ages since I asked for money for clothes. For anything. I never ask for money do I? I'm very frugal, not like some wives, spending money on everything and nothing, I'm not like that, so please Vincent, just this once

VINCENT gives her a look that cuts her off.

Enter CARLA.

| CARLA | You wouldn't believe tonight, Mum. I was in Cassanova's earlier. It were dead quiet for a Friday night. Hardly anybody going out these days, even with the two-for-one vodkas. I'm at the bar when Kylie Phillips comes over, the one from My Mark's media |

	class. Alright Dad? She comes up to me with a right look on her. So I'm like, who's pissed in your drink?
JOY	Carla
VINCENT	Good girl.
JOY	language.
CARLA	Kylie's all "Why've you been spreading shit 'bout me?"
JOY	Again…
CARLA	So I said, "I haven't been spreading shit 'bout you, your tits *are* saggy." She had nothing, no come back. Game, set and match to Carla. You only just back from work Dad? Teach her to eye up My Mark. I've seen her, soon as she think my back's turned she's all over him like carrot on puke. She keeps doing that I'll smack her.
JOY	Carla, please…
VINCENT	Too right. Take no nonsense.
CARLA	I will Mum, I promise you. Dad, them rats kept me awake all last night.
JOY	I've said to your Dad
CARLA	You want to get some poison.

JOY	to get some poison.
CARLA	They're having a right party up there. It's disgusting.
JOY	I'll phone the council tomorrow.
VINCENT	You will not.
JOY	Least they might do something.
VINCENT	You'll leave it to me. I've already had a look.
JOY	They can send someone round.
VINCENT	I will sort it. I don't want the council round here. Do you hear me? You know what they're like! You have them snooping round here they'll tax us for the clouds.
JOY	You're at work
VINCENT	You'll do what I tell you.
JOY	all day.
VINCENT	I said no. That's that.
CARLA	I've had a night out and I come home and he's only just back from the 'office'.
VINCENT	There's a lot on.
CARLA	Murderer.
JOY	Not again you two.

CARLA	Not enough time in the day to be killing all the little animals, you have to go through the night, is that it?
JOY	It's late.
CARLA	All them sheep need their throats cut, don't they Dad? Too many of them anyway.
VINCENT	You should lay off the drink, girl.
CARLA	Baa baa black sheep have you any / wool?
VINCENT	/ lentils?
CARLA	No actually I haven't, but how about turning me into a shepherd's pie?
VINCENT	It gives you a mouth.
JOY	Think about that poor, poor
CARLA	How many was it today, Dad? Five hundred, a thousand?
VINCENT	*(AN INSULT) Vegetarian.*
CARLA	Don't want anything dead on my plate.
VINCENT	You like your cornflakes.
CARLA	So?
VINCENT	All the poor little boy calves. Can't make any milk. Do you think they get sent to the seaside?

CARLA	That's different.
VINCENT	A dead cow's a dead cow.
CARLA	Meat's chopping down the rainforests and it's why Mary Banks is too lardy to get a boyfriend.
JOY	Mary Banks? Joyce's girl, she used to be such a thin
CARLA	She smells of cheeseburgers.
JOY	a thin one.
CARLA	Whole word's becoming a fatso cos of you.
VINCENT	Nothing wrong with it.
CARLA	You'll end up a lard-arse.
VINCENT	Joy. You need to sort that girl out.
CARLA	A big, fat belly.
VINCENT	Thinks she can say what she likes.
CARLA	A huge, humungous, beachball belly.
VINCENT	To her own father.
CARLA	A ginormous, belt busting-
JOY	Carla! Stop it, love. With all that's happened how can you argue at a time like this?
CARLA	Time like what?
VINCENT	She means that lad that got himself killed.

CARLA	Rob? You didn't even know him.
VINCENT	I know.
JOY	It's upset everyone.
CARLA	You wouldn't have liked him if you did.
VINCENT	I've told her this.
JOY	As a mother
CARLA	Once in geography class
JOY	I can feel the loss
CARLA	he tried to throw Mr Henderson out the fourth floor window.
VINCENT	What did I tell you, woman?
CARLA	Got himself kicked out for fighting.
JOY	Who with?
CARLA	Er, everyone.
VINCENT	No good. No good to man nor beast.
JOY	You knew him?
CARLA	He asked me out.
VINCENT	You didn't?
JOY	You?
CARLA	So nervous he was shaking.
JOY	You and he
VINCENT	You shouldn't be hanging around with lads like that.

JOY	were an item?
VINCENT	Lucky he didn't get you pregnant.
CARLA	Dad! He was alright - really sweet. When he asked me out his face was like a cherry.
VINCENT	You didn't.

BEAT.

CARLA	Is it a problem if I did?
JOY	You must be so
VINCENT	This, Joy, this is your influence.
JOY	so, so
CARLA	He was alright looking.
JOY	upset.
VINCENT	I expected better.
CARLA	Not my type though.
JOY	Oh. Oh.
CARLA	Sweet though. Once.
JOY	Did you ever meet his Mum?
CARLA	Once or twice. Round theirs, ages ago.
JOY	You know the family. Vincent, she knows the family.
CARLA	I didn't hardly ever talk to them.
JOY	They would remember you, I'm sure they'd remember you.

CARLA	It was ages ago.
JOY	Sandra would remember.
CARLA	Who's Sandra?
JOY	We should -Robert's Mother -we should go round to pay our condolences, we should. Sandra would remember.
VINCENT	You don't go round there.
JOY	We've got to pay our respects.
VINCENT	I am telling you
CARLA	Yeah, yeah, why not?
VINCENT	no, because
CARLA	Mum's right, we should.
VINCENT	Do not go round to that house.
JOY	But
VINCENT	I've told you.
CARLA	I'm going.
VINCENT	You are not.
CARLA	Maybe you can get away ordering her about, but not me. I'm going.
JOY	She's practically an old girlfriend, Vincent. Sandra would appreciate
VINCENT	No.
CARLA	Yeah.

JOY	it, I'm sure.
VINCENT	No one from this family is to have anything to do with them.
JOY	But Sandra must be, it must be awful
VINCENT	You are not going.
JOY	terrible, especially knowing the killer's still out there.
VINCENT	That's that.
CARLA	He isn't.
VINCENT	What?
CARLA	They've found the bastard - Chrissy Hinton. It's all round town.
VINCENT	Chrissy Hinton? Nonsense.
JOY	He always was a strange one.
VINCENT	Chrissy's alright.
CARLA	There's a crowd outside his house, shouting, throwing bottles. Loads of police trying to stop it proper kicking-off.
JOY	Still living at home with his Mum in his forties.
CARLA	He lives at home, at *forty*?
JOY	Those like him often do.

VINCENT	Chrissy's a bit soft in the head. But no one can believe he's a killer.
JOY	If they've arrested him, the police
VINCENT	Real gentle lad.
JOY	must have a reason, and those sorts, you can't be sure of them can you? They need an eye kept on them, can't control themselves.
VINCENT	He's been arrested?
CARLA	Yeah.
VINCENT	Why's the crowd outside his house then?
JOY	The community has a right
VINCENT	To scare an old lady?
JOY	to be upset, think of Sandra, we have to go and see her.
CARLA	We'll go tomorrow.
JOY	That poor, poor boy.
VINCENT	Leave that Sandra woman well alone.
CARLA	We're going.
VINCENT	While you're in my house
CARLA	It'll be good to get away from the stink of those animals, it gets on everything in this house. We're goin' round to see…

JOY	Sandra.
CARLA	Sandra, and we're goin' to that funeral.
VINCENT	Listen, madam
CARLA	Everyone's going. Everyone. You can sit here on your own and they'll all wonder why you're not there.

PAUSE.

CARLA	I'm off to bed – my head is spinning...I shouldn't have had that last double.

Exit CARLA.

JOY	Carla, Carla knew him, Vincent, we, we should go.

Exit JOY.

VINCENT	I watch them get ready. Like they're organising a street party. Pigs at the trough of tragedy. All these people who gossip about each other. Who slip knives into each other's backs every day. Neighbours throwing dog turds into each

other's gardens. Smiling at each other across the fence the next day. Being jealous. Being stuck up. All these people brought together by the death. Of you.

*Enter **ROB**, swigging from a bottle of beer.*

Funny. How popular you become when you're dead. Rob this. Rob that. Not much use now eh? Shame they weren't all so interested before. It's like everyone wakes up. For a moment. They realise how important life is. When tragedy strikes. Family jumps to the top of the list. "We'll spend more time together", I'll stop shouting", "I won't hate the way you breathe". Till tomorrow. Till they forget again.

*Enter **JOY** and **CARLA**. They undress and change into funeral clothes.*

I washed Joy. In the early days. Can you imagine that? Spent hours in the bath together. I'd wash her. Following the veins around her body. She felt smooth and strong. Never done that with anyone before. Hands shook the first time. Made her giggle. Her skin was so bright and alive.

JOY and CARLA are ready.

If you know what you're doing. You can take the skin off a pig in one big piece.

ROB crouches in a corner, watches.

JOY   I know, it's so sad. So sad that Maggie isn't here, her poor Roy, I hope he's alright...you say that Doreen, but any operation is a dangerous thing...I'm sure he'll be fine. She will, she'll be heartbroken...I didn't try and back out, no, I wanted to be here, for Sandra, in bits she was, absolute bits...I didn't try and back out, something came up, Doreen, beyond my control...I didn't feel so well anymore, that's all...I'm here now aren't I?

VINCENT Look at your Mother. Celebrity Sandra. But where was she? Nobody's asking her

	that. Where was she when you were causing bother? Insulting people. Any kind of mother she'd have been sorting you out. Right out.
CARLA	You're his Uncle? I went to school with him, yeah? We had science together. Stars an' all that. I was never that good at it...Rob loved it – the bull, the ram......that's it, the conste, the consolations, well into it...before he went all...I went to school with him, that's how I knew him.
JOY	I wasn't expecting all those cameras, were you Doreen, hundreds of them all flashing, like a film premiere? It's not right. They can smell death those people, drawn to it so they can take their pictures, scuttling around like rats.
BEAT.	
	I don't know if we'll be on the news Doreen, no...I don't think I want to...you're recording it are you....once in a lifetime chance to get on the TV, but on

the news Doreen…it'll be you, paedophiles and murderers…Joyce Banks? What's Joyce Banks got to do…it's not the same dress…

VINCENT   Best for all concerned. Now you've gone. No lads causing bother outside the shop. Streets quiet at night. Peaceful. People-

ROB spins the bottle on the floor.

- people should be glad.

CARLA   I'm really…yeah, I'm really sorry…Rob was…you shouldn't say that 'bout him, you're his Uncle…he was alright, he was, you shouldn't…I didn't know…I didn't know that, but he…at school he…he was alright, not my type, right, he did ask me out once…you should have seen him, his face was like strawberry jam…so upset when I said no, he was al…well, I've done that, not proper stealing, but from her purse, a couple of quid for a fag…not proper…I'd heard he'd beaten a lad…he used to be so gentle, he was this really sweet - he was, I'm telling you he was…I didn't say you was wrong...I'm not saying I knew him better, but....but at school he was really...he was...he wasn't always like that...I don't want to argue with you - but I will...

JOY   Carla, sssshh! *(To DOREEN)* It's not exactly the same dress is it? It's similar, Doreen, but it's not the same. Yes, I've had this one a while, but a funeral is not the place for a new dress...yours is very nice, factory outlet is it? Did you see the outside of Chrissy Hinton's house...the 'Bring Back Hanging' signs? It would be a good idea if people just calmed down and waited to find out what happened...you helped paint them?...Yes, I heard, I heard that Derek Standford phoned the police and volunteered to be the hangman...yes, yes, Derek is very public spirited. But as Vincent says...Vincent said the man hasn't actually been found guilty of anything...you're right Doreen, often there is no smoke without fire, but we should wait and see, don't you think?

VINCENT　　Joy, shush!

JOY　　I wish Vincent had made more of an effort, he looks so scruffy. When we met he was always so smart. Used to take longer to get ready than I did. He'd say he wanted to look good for me. I wanted him to wear his nice coat, he has a lovely coat, but will he wear it?

VINCENT　　It'll all blow over soon. Once the funeral's out of the way. It'll blow over. Already starting to. Even Joy's had enough of you. Yesterday she decides she doesn't want to come today. After all that fuss. Said she felt ill. Sickened by this circus I should imagine. Shame Doreen turned up to give us a lift.

JOY　　*(WHISPERS)* They're bringing Robert in, I mean the coffin...watch Sandra, Doreen, watch her...there she goes. I knew her legs wouldn't last, the poor woman. Have you been round her house? It's...well it's a council house…nothing wrong with that, no…dust everywhere…

VINCENT Carried down the aisle like it's a state funeral. By your pack of mates. Course, they're making a mess of it. Coffin's wobbling. They're fidgeting under the weight. You young lads. Can't do a job properly. None of you look so cocky now.

ROB spins the bottle again.

The whole church goes hush. People anemic in their grief for someone they barely knew. The crying starts.

JOY Sandra started it, did you see Doreen, now it's flowing across the church…should we be crying Doreen? Should we…do you want a tissue, I've some in my handbag…no, no I don't feel like crying…it doesn't seem to want to come.

CARLA I didn't mean…don't cry it's…I'm not good with…I know he was your nephew…all I meant was, listen, right, I said listen…do you remember him when he was twelve or thirteen he was…but he was...he was wasn't he? That's how he really was...his Dad? I didn't know he'd died? I didn't know...he was alright, Rob...don't cry, I'm...I'm really...sorry...

JOY   I am upset, I am, but I'm trying to be strong for Sandra...I'll be no use to her if I'm all teary will I...don't think about yourself Doreen.

VINCENT   Hang on. We're at the wrong funeral. "A brave, faithful and loved son"? Vicar never met you then.

JOY   It's called being strong Doreen, strong...what would you have been like with the rats in our loft yesterday...rats, Doreen, don't be so squeamish, you're never more than six feet away from one so they say. You look pale, are you alright? I had to be strong. I wasn't having rats running around, so I did some investigating. I went up there, I wanted to see what they got up to.

VINCENT   "But as for the cowardly, the faithless, the detestable, as for murderers, their portion will be in the lake that burns with fire and sulphur, which is the second death." See what you've done lad? Got everyone pouring hellfire on Chrissy. They know nothing.

*PAUSE – suddenly **ROB** smashes the bottle, holds the shard as a weapon.*

It's too late to be upset by death, Sandra. Too late. Your Mother can weep for the crowd as they help her out of the church. But it was time. A matter of time. Before you hurt someone. Not now, lad. Not now. It's over.

CARLA   He's really dead isn't he? I know it's been two weeks, but I hadn't thought...he's really dead.

JOY   I could hear those rats in the roof above our bedroom, running around all night. Vincent? He's been working hard, Vincent's been, Vincent is...I don't know...Here he is. I was telling Doreen you've been working long hours, Vincent.

VINCENT   We should go.

JOY   Very long hours…I thought, well that's it; there must be something up there, attracting them.

VINCENT I told you that I'd-

JOY   -you were working and I hate rats, hate them. I wanted them gone, so I put on my rubber gloves…it's not about being brave Doreen, I just hate rats – I put on my rubber gloves and went up there.

BEAT.

And there it was – a coat, a blue coat stuffed behind the chimney breast.

BEAT.

I don't know Doreen, I don't know why anyone would stuff a coat behind the chimney, no idea at all. What do you think Vincent? Do you have any idea? Because it was a nice coat once, you could tell, a nice blue coat, but not anymore, with the dirt, and the stains. All the stains.

VINCENT Joy-

JOY   -made me retch.

VINCENT Joy-

JOY   - I'm ready to go now.

ROB puts his hood up.

Skin

VINCENT   Threw my guts up on the first day. They
took me out on the kill floor. Only been
there an hour. Brought this pig in.
Stunned it. Stuck it. Right in front of me.
On the job training meant something then.
And they watched me. As the blood
drained from the pig. I felt the colour drain
from my face. One lad shoved a bucket at
me. I nearly filled it. All I heard when I
went to bed that night was pigs squealing.

*Enter **ROB**.*

"Don't worry, mate. You'll get used to it."
Never thought I would. Never. I buried it
inside me. Couldn't bear to think about it.
Only way to keep going. Three months
later – it's just a job.

*As **VINCENT** talks **ROB** struts about, shadow boxing,
staring at **VINCENT**, getting in VINCENT'S face, trying to
intimidate and distract him.*

VINCENT   When I started. Four of us would kill and dress the animal. You had to know the different types of knife. The different cuts. We'd work quietly. Slowly preparing the animal. Each one of us able to do every part of it. There was skill. Technique. Then the slaughterhouse gets bought up by a big company. Big ideas. Big machines. They don't want us to do the whole job anymore. They want us to be one tiny bit. "More efficient." It's not a slaughterhouse. It's a car production line. And the line gets faster. Faster. Quota's always going up. I keep up. Don't get me wrong. I keep up no problem. I do a good job. Can take whatever they throw at me. But it's fast. This line stretching on and on. Full of animals. Forever. And me. This one knife on it. Cutting and cutting. Over and over. Sometimes I don't even remember being there. Wake up at the end of my shift. Only part of my brain working is the bit connected to the knife. Sticking again and again. Five, six hundred animals a day. There or there abouts. Two and a half thousand a week. Not including overtime. Over a hundred thousand a year. For seventeen years. One and a half million or more. Practically a city's worth. The line moves so fast. So fast. It used to be the priests who slaughtered the animals. Sacrificing to the gods. It had honour. Prestige. Now? We're hidden away. Kept out of sight. For fear of someone getting upset by what we do.

ROB *gets right in* *VINCENT'S* *face one last time,* *VINCENT* *cannot look at* *ROB.*

Enter *JOY.*

Exit *ROB.*

VINCENT	It's a shock.
JOY	A what?
VINCENT	A shock. For you.
JOY	A bit of a shock?

VINCENT	Yes.
JOY	A shock?
VINCENT	For you.
JOY	The boy's dead
VINCENT	He is.
JOY	of course it's a, it's a big shock, a big, yes, yes it is.
VINCENT	I understand.
JOY	I wasn't expecting
VINCENT	I know.
JOY	I wasn't expecting you to have
VINCENT	I know.
JOY	I wasn't expecting that you had...the boy.
VINCENT	I know that.
JOY	Are you sure.
VINCENT	Of?
JOY	That you
VINCENT	Yes.
JOY	Couldn't you be mistaken, because you're not a doctor, maybe
VINCENT	Joy...
JOY	listen, listen to me, maybe you didn't kill him, you just hurt him

VINCENT	Just a scratch?
JOY	yes, exactly, you just hurt him and he was still alive
VINCENT	Wounded.
JOY	wounded, that's right, but still alive, and then, and then
VINCENT	And then what, Joy?
JOY	and then, oh shit. Language, Joy, language.
VINCENT	It will be okay.
JOY	Remain calm, Joy.
VINCENT	I am telling you. It will be okay.
JOY	That boy is dead by your hand.
VINCENT	I had no choice.
JOY	Everyone's going berserk out there, the papers are saying
VINCENT	Don't listen to what the papers
JOY	that it had to be someone like Hinton
VINCENT	Leave Chrissy alone.
JOY	and all the time it's you, it's you who murdered that boy.
VINCENT	Killed.
JOY	What?

VINCENT	I killed him.
JOY	I said, I just said
VINCENT	Murdered. I didn't murder him. I killed him.
JOY	Wha, what does it matter, what's, I don't understand what you're, what?
VINCENT	Murder means it was wrong.
JOY	The boy is dead Vincent.
VINCENT	I *was* there.
JOY	The boy is dead.
VINCENT	You keep saying that.
JOY	He's dead, of course it's
VINCENT	Wrong?
JOY	Yes.
VINCENT	Why?
JOY	Because, you don't kill.
VINCENT	It isn't wrong.
JOY	Of course it is.
VINCENT	Why?
JOY	Because this is about the shop.
VINCENT	That was the start of it.
JOY	That boy is dead because of what happened outside the shop.

VINCENT	I will not be spoken to like that.
JOY	A grubby little fight because of what happened outside the shop, and you go and
VINCENT	He attacked me. Ambushed me.
JOY	You could have run away.
VINCENT	Run from that little…no. I couldn't. No way.
JOY	If only you had.
VINCENT	There would have been no end to it. Can't show weakness to his type.
JOY	Was it quick?
VINCENT	It happened quickly.
JOY	The boy didn't
VINCENT	It was quick.
JOY	he didn't suffer?
VINCENT	Like. Like the abattoir.
JOY	Did he suffer Vincent, please, I couldn't bear
VINCENT	Like the abattoir. One cut. I promise.
JOY	I don't want the details, it makes me, the thought of…yes or no only.

BEAT.

VINCENT	No.

47

JOY	Thank god.
VINCENT	He didn't suffer. I know what I'm doing.
JOY	It was self-defence?
VINCENT	Yes.
JOY	He attacked you?
VINCENT	I told you.
JOY	You had no choice?
VINCENT	That's what I said.
JOY	But
VINCENT	No buts, Joy.
JOY	But you've got
VINCENT	What?
JOY	you've got, sometimes Vincent, not all the time, I'm not saying it's all the time, but sometimes
VINCENT	Spit it out.
JOY	you've got a temper.
VINCENT	*(ANGRY)* I have *(NORMAL)* I did not kill that lad because I was angry.
JOY	No?
VINCENT	No.
JOY	You're sure?
VINCENT	I don't like repeating myself.

JOY	No. Only
VINCENT	What?
JOY	It's just
VINCENT	What?
JOY	why didn't you call the police?
VINCENT	Call the
JOY	Because you would, wouldn't you, if you'd been attacked, you'd call the
VINCENT	Too late. Once he was dead.
JOY	if you do the right thing, you call the police, because
VINCENT	Don't need them.
JOY	because you've done the right thing
VINCENT	I will not be judged by people.
JOY	and so you need to tell someone
VINCENT	Deciding what's right and wrong.
JOY	tell them that you've done the right thing
VINCENT	I know I did.
JOY	so everyone can say that you've done the right thing.
VINCENT	That's all I need.
PAUSE.	
JOY	If only you'd called the police.

VINCENT	Think, woman. I'm in an empty car park. It's late. Dark. There's no one else about. I'm covered in blood. A dead idiot at my feet. A hole in his neck. No one saw what happened. No one saw him attack me. My word against his dead body. They'd lock me up for a thousand years.
JOY	Yes, yes, you're right.
VINCENT	Doesn't matter if anyone else knows. Doesn't matter what anyone else believes. I had no choice, Joy.
JOY	He didn't suffer?
VINCENT	It was quick.
JOY	Yes.
VINCENT	Do you believe me?
JOY	It's, it's a shock, a big...what about Chrissy Hinton?
VINCENT	He didn't do anything. Sooner or later the police will realise that.
JOY	They've had him for over a week.
VINCENT	Funeral was yesterday. They'll wait till it calms down. Quietly let him go.
JOY	Poor Chrissy.

VINCENT	He'll be alright. Everything will calm down. A few weeks. Couple of months. It will be okay. People will forget. You know what it's like. Newspapers will forget. Won't be on the TV. It'll be the next tragedy. No one really cares. Things will go back to normal.
JOY	Vincent
VINCENT	They will Joy. You and I. We'll go back. To how we've always been. Normal.
JOY	Normal?
VINCENT	Everything will be the same. In a little while. We stay quiet. Stay quiet and
JOY	Roy's got cancer of the pancreas.
VINCENT	calm.
JOY	Maggie's Roy, Maggie Sharp, it's not his gall bladder, it's cancer of the pancreas. Doreen told me, swore me to secrecy. It's terrible. Roy's not that long left Doreen says. Where is your pancreas, is it in your intestines?
VINCENT	Behind your stomach.

JOY	Maggie's very upset apparently, very upset. Says she'll change the living room wallpaper when Roy's gone, she's never liked the pattern he chose last time they had it done, says it looks dowdy. Poor Maggie, she told Doreen that life would never be the same again. I think we need new wallpaper in our living room.
VINCENT	This isn't the time.
JOY	It looks dowdy.
VINCENT	Couple of years left in that yet.
JOY	I look dowdy.
VINCENT	You've had a shock.
JOY	I feel dowdy.
VINCENT	A week or two.
JOY	I hate it.
VINCENT	Everything will be back to normal.
JOY	I'm forty, only just forty, I could pass for late thirties I'm sure, if I didn't look dowdy. I don't want to feel like this.
VINCENT	I promise.
JOY	I want some new wallpaper.
VINCENT	Don't I always take care of everything?

JOY	I want new clothes.
VINCENT	Leave it to me.
JOY	I shouldn't have to ask for things, Vincent.
VINCENT	We can't go splashing out now.
JOY	I shouldn't have to have to beg for the things I would like.
VINCENT	Need to be normal.
JOY	I have a right to have the things that I would like, you make me plead for the smallest thing and I don't, I don't, it's not something that I like
VINCENT	People would wonder.
JOY	no, it's not, so from now on, I've decided. It's not going to happen anymore, not now, do you understand, it's not going to happen anymore and I want, I want
VINCENT	You've no idea.
JOY	What I want is...,yes, I want the credit card. To get what I want when I choose to
VINCENT	I'm not giving you-
JOY	I'm, I'm in charge, yes, don't smile, I'm in charge now, you understand. I'm in charge

	because of what you did, you'll do what I say
VINCENT	Or?
JOY	or I'll tell the police, I'll tell…I'll phone them up and tell them that you killed that poor, poor boy.
VINCENT	I'm your husband.
JOY	I know, that's why I'm doing this.

PAUSE.

VINCENT	No.
JOY	No?
VINCENT	No.
JOY	You have to.
VINCENT	No.
JOY	Or I'll call
VINCENT	You don't have it in you.
JOY	I do, I can do it right
VINCENT	You won't. You'll sit tight. Stay quiet. We won't mention this again.
JOY	Vincent
VINCENT	That's that.

Enter CARLA.

CARLA	Lads are idiots. Totally deluded, baked beans for brains idiots. My Mark – what a tool. You ask him why you haven't heard from him for few days, just a question, nothing heavy, just askin', and he's off – "I need my own space, you know, I can't be with you all the time." Like, like I'm always on his back. As if. As if I would be that needy. But then, right, when you, when you're not at their feet telling them how wonderful they are every second of every day, when you're not worshipping them and they're not in control, then something's wrong – you're the weird one for having something else to do. And now, now he's got the hump because I wouldn't go round there. He gets his space whenever he wants, but all I've got is some idiot who thinks he's Jesus. All because I wouldn't go round his this afternoon cos I wanted to watch Hinton's house burn down instead. What a tool.
VINCENT	Burnt?

CARLA	To. The. Ground.
JOY	No.
CARLA	It was brilliant. We all cheered as the flames took over. Everyone was there, even Kylie Slagging Philips. With her radioactive spray-tan, and a smile on her face like she knows something I don't.
VINCENT	How did it happen?
CARLA	An act of God. My money's on Darren Ferguson. If he did, he's a hero.
JOY	Chrissy's Mum's alright though, isn't she?
VINCENT	But why?
CARLA	His hair Dad, we don't like the way he does his hair.
VINCENT	What?
CARLA	Cos he's murdering scum.
VINCENT	Chrissy hasn't done anything.
CARLA	He's been arrested.
VINCENT	Arrested. Arrested. Not been to court. Not found guilty.
CARLA	They wouldn't have arrested him if they didn't think he'd done it.
JOY	She's okay?

VINCENT	Nobody's proved he did it.
CARLA	Everybody knows he did it.
VINCENT	You can't just decide.
CARLA	The last few years, this town's been on it's arse. Now it's finally doing something. We're not waiting for the police to sort it out. We want something done now.
VINCENT	Who's 'we'?
CARLA	The people out there.
VINCENT	We're having a revolution. That's what's happening?
JOY	Did you see Chrissy's Mum?
CARLA	What are we supposed to do, let him get away with it? We want justice.
VINCENT	By burning his house down?
CARLA	He can't come back here now.
JOY	Was she in the house?
VINCENT	It's not right.
CARLA	Hinton should suffer.
JOY	Was his Mum in the house?
VINCENT	What if he didn't do it?
CARLA	You know what he was like.

VINCENT	Yes. Simple Chrissy. Butt of everyone's jokes.
JOY	Answer me! When they burnt the house down, was his Mum
CARLA	Yes.
JOY	Oh my hell.
VINCENT	She can't be.
JOY	They've killed Madge Hinton, Vincent they've
VINCENT	She can't.
JOY	This isn't happening.
CARLA	But they got her out.
VINCENT	Hell's teeth Carla!
CARLA	What?
JOY	She's really
VINCENT	Why didn't you say she was alive?
JOY	really alright
CARLA	I just did.
JOY	really okay, I mean she's alive?
CARLA	She looked a bit upset.
JOY	Thank all the lucky, lucky
CARLA	I'm just sorry Hinton wasn't in that house when the roof fell in. Two weeks ago Rob

was walking about. Alive. Breathing. Thinking. Now he doesn't exist anymore – and what the fuck is that all about, yeah? What. The. Fuck?

JOY   Carla, Lang-

CARLA   Hinton gets away with it, what's to stop him doing it to someone else? To any of us? To me? He should be burnt alive until there's nothing left, but ash.

VINCENT   What's wrong with you?

CARLA   What's wrong with you?

JOY   We're fine then, if Madge Hinton's alright, then we're okay.

CARLA   You care more about Hinton than Rob.

VINCENT   Chrissy's a good lad. A hundred times better than your Rob.

CARLA   You should be careful.

JOY   Besides, the house was rented.

CARLA   People would be angry if they heard what you just said.

VINCENT   That lad was a waste of space.

CARLA	Michael Crossley had dogshit pushed through his letterbox cos he said Rob was a thug.
VINCENT	Finally. Some sense.
JOY	They can rent some place new.
CARLA	He had his car keyed and his kitchen window smashed.
VINCENT	I hope the police find who did it.
CARLA	I don't think you do.
PAUSE.	
CARLA	I don't think you do and I don't like what you say about Rob. He was alright, I knew him, you didn't. I knew him. People aren't allowed to say these things about him anymore, he's dead, it's not very nice. I'm going to make sure no one forgets about Rob. I'm collecting money for a memorial so that people remember him everyday. And they remember Hinton should burn.

Exit CARLA.

JOY	I don't even need to tell the police, do I? I could tell that lot out there.
VINCENT	There was nothing else I could do, Joy.
JOY	Do you think they'll believe you now? I could tell Doreen. She's like the plague that woman, running from door to door spreading the good news. The whole town would know by teatime.
VINCENT	Didn't know they'd burn Chrissy's house down. Didn't know Carla would...
JOY	And what do you think they'd do to you if they found out? They're on the rampage and they'd have you in bits, absolute bits before the police could even arrest you. Look at what you've done to us...I will have that credit card.
VINCENT	Wasn't supposed to be like this.
JOY	I think it's best if you sleep in the spare room from now on. I won't have you in our bed.
VINCENT	He wouldn't stop, Joy.
JOY	it shouldn't make much difference, we hardly...

VINCENT   I tried to make him

JOY   I hate lying there with the stink of the animals in the room no matter how many times you

VINCENT   But he wouldn't-

JOY   -and don't interrupt me Vincent, don't interrupt me because I will not have it, do you understand me? I don't like it, I have things to say Vincent, important things and you will listen.

PAUSE.

JOY   I'll nip into town at the weekend for a spot of shopping. I'll have to have a think about what to buy. It's been such a long time since I looked nice. Maybe, maybe I'll get a leather jacket; I used to have a leather jacket years ago. I loved being all wrapped up in it, felt protected. Maybe I'll get one.

PAUSE.

JOY   You don't mind, do you?

PAUSE.

62

JOY   You don't mind, Vincent? I really wouldn't want you to mind.

BEAT.

VINCENT   No.

JOY   Good, that's all settled then.

*Enter **ROB**, head down.*

VINCENT   Now then big man.

ROB   The butcher, thought you'd had enough?

JOY   Doreen, hello, can you hear me, the line is very crackly?

VINCENT   Not got your little mates with you tonight?

ROB   They're about.

VINCENT   Can't see them. Can't hear them. Just you and me.

ROB   You been waiting to get me on me own? Very romantic.

VINCENT   I want an apology.

JOY   That's better, I can hear you...I'm well, very well thank you. Yes, I did see you on the TV, your hair anyway...I'm nipping into town to go shopping, do you fancy...there's a what? A reenactment filmed of...that's true, you could be on TV twice in one week. I'm pleased for you.

ROB Did we scare you, that it?

VINCENT Nobody talks to me like that. Not in front of

ROB I see blokes like you all the time. Think you're hard as they come, staring us out, thinking we're chicken, but it's you that's all front. Puffing up your chest, getting all shouty.

JOY I was going to get a jacket...it is hard to believe that Chrissy Hinton could have...I know, I know the thought that someone among us could...yes Doreen, it's shocking, but I thought I'd treat myself to a leather jacket...I am not too old.

ROB But you're never gonna actually do anything. You can't. Best you can do is call the police. Or get your wife to do it.

VINCENT I don't need her to sort you out.

JOY It's about how you wear it...he might not be a murderer, Doreen, Chrissy might not

	be…you don't know what happened, no one does, that's why there's a reenactment.
ROB	You take it all right serious, don't you?
VINCENT	You are going to apologise. To me.
ROB	Cos it's just a laugh, that's all, just a big fucking ginormous laugh, but you've gone and let your feelings get hurt. Got yourself all wound up. It's been keeping you awake at night, I can tell.
JOY	Murder, murder, murder, don't go on about it, Doreen, a trip into town will take our minds off…it's dreadful it is, I know, I'm not saying…but what's done is done, life has to go on.
VINCENT	Apologise. You don't get to say these things to me. About my family. You don't get to make me look…it's not right.
ROB	I'll give you an apology.

ROB puts his hand in his pocket, pulls it out fast and aims it in VINCENT'S face.

VINCENT steps back, scared, hands up protecting his face.

ROB is standing there with nothing more threatening than his middle finger.

ROB makes slow chicken noises.

JOY   I'm not being callous. Do you remember, listen to me, do you remember how that Rob was always in trouble, it's not like he was some kind of...

VINCENT punches ROB with everything he's got, knocking him to the ground.

VINCENT stamps on ROB.

VINCENT   Ha. Ha. Fucking ha.

JOY   I'm not saying he deserved it...

VINCENT stamps on ROB again.

VINCENT   Say sorry.

ROB rolling around in pain.

JOY   No, Sandra wouldn't like it if she heard that, I wouldn't say it to her would I, but come on, remember...

VINCENT about to kick ROB.

VINCENT   Say sorry.

ROB   I had to do it, I had to or the lads'd call me
                  chicken.

VINCENT makes chicken noises, raises his foot again.

ROB   I'm sorry!

BEAT.

JOY   Everyone would be very upset to hear me
                  talking like that, yes, they would be
                  angry…yes, yes, I'm sorry Doreen, I just
                  want to go shopping…I don't know what
                  came over me…I'm sorry.

VINCENT   Not so cocky now.

VINCENT kicks ROB.

ROB scrambles away on the floor.

VINCENT pursues ROB. He has ROB cornered.

ROB   I said I was sorry! Please!

JOY   I said I'm sorry…Sandra? What, what do
                  you mean she wants to see Vincent?

VINCENT   A firm hand is what's needed. You're firm
                  with someone. They know where they
                  stand. Look at the animals. There's a
                  system with the animals. Hierarchy. Even

the chickens have a pecking order. That's
what you need.

VINCENT kicks ROB.

ROB	Please, I'm, I don't want to, I want, I want
JOY	What did Sandra say? Doreen, now don't go, why does Sandra want to see...goodbye, Doreen, goodbye.
VINCENT	You want what?
ROB	Please, me Mum, I want me Mum.

VINCENT laughs.

VINCENT feigns a kick at ROB, ROB crouches in fear.

JOY   Vincent?

VINCENT about to kick ROB.

ROB with his hands up protecting himself.

JOY	Vincent, are you listening to me?
VINCENT	Yes, Joy.
JOY	It's Sandra.
VINCENT	What about the woman?
JOY	She's coming.

VINCENT leaves ROB.

ROB picks himself up and staggers off.

VINCENT   She has no business here.

JOY   She wants to see you, today.

VINCENT   Me? Never said two words to her.

JOY   I don't like this.

VINCENT   Simple. We don't answer the door.

JOY   We can't do that.

VINCENT   Put the lock on. Turn the TV up. Sorry. Didn't hear anyone knocking.

JOY   You don't get it. You never do. She's the grieving mother, which means that right now Sandra's the Queen of this town. She can say or do anything she likes. Everyone is watching her and listening to what she says.

VINCENT   Who does she think-

JOY   -if we don't act right it will be noticed, by Doreen, by Maggie, by everyone and they'll all start looking our way wanting to know what's wrong with us, why we're

	different. Do you want the barbarians ringing the doorbell?
VINCENT	What does she want?
JOY	She could know.
VINCENT	No one knows. Except me. And you.
JOY	Maybe somebody saw you.
VINCENT	Nobody saw me.
JOY	What if they did?
VINCENT	Where's the police then?
JOY	I don't know.
VINCENT	Crashing through the windows? Where are they?
JOY	I told you I don't know, Vincent, and be nice.

BEAT.

JOY	There's no choice but to see her.
VINCENT	What do we do?
JOY	We wait.

LONG PAUSE.

VINCENT	Yesterday.
JOY	What?
VINCENT	Our wedding anniversary. Yesterday.
JOY	No it wasn't.

VINCENT	9th.
JOY	The 9th? Then it was.
VINCENT	Seventeen years.
JOY	Eighteen.

PAUSE.

VINCENT	You remember telling the parents we were getting married? Not happy.
JOY	Probably because it was the same day we told them I was pregnant.
VINCENT	Not sure who was angrier.
JOY	No.

PAUSE.

VINCENT	/ Your Dad.
JOY	My Dad. / I thought he was going to kill you.
VINCENT	Mum said I'd ruined my life.
JOY	She never did like me.
VINCENT	The wedding.
JOY	The 'Registry Office of Silence'.
VINCENT	Your Mum and Dad. Not talking to me.
JOY	Your Mum and Dad didn't speak to me.
VINCENT	No one looking at the bump.
JOY	No reception afterwards.

VINCENT	Everyone couldn't leave quick enough. Just us. Fish. Chips.
JOY	And curry sauce.
VINCENT	In that little flat.
JOY	On the other side of town.
VINCENT	Dirt cheap.
JOY	Just dirty.
VINCENT	No TV.
JOY	Only that awful sofa.
VINCENT	Thirty quid from the Sally Ann's.
JOY	The springs always stuck in your bum.
VINCENT	Just us.
JOY	And our plans.
VINCENT	Didn't matter what they thought about us. Did it? Didn't matter what they said.
JOY	Because we told each other everything then.
VINCENT	Because we were
JOY	solid.
VINCENT	Yeah.
BEAT.	
BOTH	*(SINGING)* "Solid as a rock!"
PAUSE.	

*Enter **CARLA** with **SANDRA**.*

***SANDRA** cast in shadow.*

JOY	Shame.
CARLA	Mum, Dad it's
JOY	Sandra love, it's so good to see you. Come in, come in, sorry I haven't been round, but I thought you would have so many visitors and I didn't want to crowd you. You haven't met my husband Vincent have you? This is Vincent, my husband.
VINCENT	Sandra. Sorry. For your loss.
JOY	It's so good that you've come to see us. Vincent and I have been thinking, you've been in our thoughts lots and lots, and it's really good to see you, really, yes.

PAUSE.

CARLA	I've got something for you. It's for Rob, I've been
JOY	How have you been? No, don't listen to me, that's, I shouldn't have, that's a stupid thing to say, it's so very difficult to know what to say in these situations isn't it? Because you feel you need to say

something and to say nothing would be the worst thing, but then you're always so scared that you'll say the wrong thing and upset the other person. It's hard to find words that are appropriate. Forgive me…

PAUSE.

CARLA   I've been round nearly everybody, and I've not got as much as I hoped, but

JOY   It is lovely to see you, lovely, lovely, very, I should have come and seen you, I know, and what, with the, why are you here?

SANDRA   I've been to the shop.

VINCENT   The shop?

JOY   Did Mr Patel say…?

VINCENT   Did he?

JOY   It was over and done with very quickly, Sandra, very quick.

VINCENT   Patel…I had a run-in with your lad.

JOY   They were giving Vincent a real hard time.

VINCENT   Outside the shop. Rob and his mates acting tough. He had a mouth on him. But then he was always causing bother. What

	kind of lad gets himself in that kind of trouble? That's what I want to
JOY	Vincent.

BEAT.

VINCENT	Joy's right. Not the sort of thing a mother wants to hear about her son.
JOY	It was lucky no one got hurt.
SANDRA	I went to see Mr Henderson.
VINCENT	Who?
CARLA	Our old geography
SANDRA	And I spoke to Mr Patel, about what Rob said.
JOY	I know, Mr Patel was ever so upset when Rob called him that, ever so.
SANDRA	I've visited all the people Rob ever...
VINCENT	Why?

BEAT.

SANDRA	I know, I know my boy was no angel. Everyone round here thinks I'm a fool. I know. He kept getting into...and I tried to stop it. I really did, but after his Dad died the more I held on to him, the more he slipped through my fingers.

BEAT.

	I wanted to say I'm sorry.
JOY	About the shop?
SANDRA	I'm sorry.

BEAT.

VINCENT	I accept your apology. On behalf of your son.
CARLA	I got you five hundred quid, I'm pretty pleased actually.
VINCENT	Thank you Sandra. Thank you.
JOY	It's very kind of you to think of us, very kind indeed and I'm so glad that you came here, Sandra, but please, you've said enough, this must be such a tough time for you and you shouldn't be worrying about us, it's important you take care of yourself. Is there someone waiting for you at home...Doreen? Maggie? Good old Maggie, you can always rely on her. Poor Roy, poor, poor Roy...
CARLA	I've got it all here in a bread bag, I didn't know what else to put it in.

JOY	Thank you for coming, really and I'll pop round soon, I promise, thank you, you take care now, I'll see
VINCENT	Was he a good lad? Your Rob?
JOY	I said we'll see Sandra later.
VINCENT	Was he a good lad? When he was younger?
JOY	Vincent, this isn't helping.
VINCENT	Our Carla keeps telling us how wonderful he was.
CARLA	Dad!
JOY	I don't want, Sandra doesn't want to hear this.

BEAT.

SANDRA	Such a kind little boy. All smiles and hugs.
VINCENT	He was, was he? Kids are a lot of fun when they're little, aren't they? The world hasn't got a grip on them yet. Remember those days, Sandra. Remember them. Leave what happened outside the shop to me.
JOY	You listen to Vincent, I'm sure he's finished talking now, haven't you Vincent?

	Now make sure you go home and get some rest.
SANDRA	I can't sleep.
JOY	I'm sure, I'm sure sleep is hard to come by, has the Doctor given you...
SANDRA	When I close my eyes all I see is his body.
JOY	Don't, don't think of that.
SANDRA	When I identified my son.
JOY	I didn't know you'd...

PAUSE.

SANDRA	With all the holes in him.
JOY	Holes?

PAUSE.

JOY	Holes?

PAUSE.

JOY	But I thought
CARLA	That bastard Hinton.
JOY	I thought you said, that people said
CARLA	And he's still saying he didn't do it.
JOY	that it was quick? I thought
CARLA	Give him a kicking until he confesses I say.
JOY	it was just one, Sandra, I didn't know...

CARLA   I'd do it if they gave me the chance. That's why I got you all the money. Like I said, I'd hoped to get more, but I did alright, even got twenty quid out of Sherri Riverford and she won't even give to Children in Need cos she says she hates kids. It's for a memorial. Like a statue of Rob, or a bench. People always get benches don't they, you could get a bench with his name on. One of those little plaques and that way people won't ever forget what happened.

SANDRA   I want to forget.

CARLA   You can't, I've collected all this money, what do I do with it if you don't want it?

SANDRA   I want to forget everything.

SANDRA fades to darkness.

CARLA   This isn't just about you, this is about all of us round here, we want justice. We want Hinton hanging from a lamppost and we want to remember Rob. Lots of people have put in and you've got to take it, you've

VINCENT	Carla.
CARLA	But it's for Rob.
VINCENT	Let her go.
CARLA	You've got to.
VINCENT	Goodbye Sandra.
CARLA	What am I supposed to do with it all?

Exit CARLA.

PAUSE.

VINCENT	People don't want to know how things really happen. They don't want to see what happens behind the factory walls. In the shadows.
JOY	You said it was one cut.
VINCENT	You would have got queasy.
JOY	You said it was quick.
VINCENT	I stopped his suffering.
JOY	He wasn't supposed to have suffered at all.
VINCENT	Can't stick something and there not be a little suffering.
JOY	What if it was our Carla?

VINCENT	I had to kill him.
JOY	I'm going to the police
VINCENT	I wanted to tell you what happened
JOY	right now
VINCENT	but I knew what everyone would think of me. Every headline. Every newspaper - "Slaughterman slaughters poor, poor boy."
JOY	I will not be that woman on the TV, the wife saying she never knew as they pull more and more bodies out of the ground, and everyone's thinking, "Of course she knew."
VINCENT	You do know.
JOY	No I didn't! No! I should have gone to the police as soon as I found the coat, but I thought, I've been married to him for eighteen years he can't be a murderer, he can't be, he used to be this warm and kind man and you can't be like that and a killer can you, so I thought there must be some reason.
VINCENT	He attacked me. I had no-

JOY	Stop saying that! You told me, you told me...but you butchered him......I need to go, I need, I can't breathe
VINCENT	Do you ever think of the plans we made? In that little flat.
JOY	I need to go, the police I must go to the police.
VINCENT	The house we were going to live in. By the seaside.
JOY	I need my coat, do I, my, forget the coat, Joy, forget the coat just go, go
VINCENT	You ever think of the house by the seaside Joy?
JOY	go now.
VINCENT	Joy!
BEAT.	
JOY	It's what's kept me here all these years.
VINCENT	Our house. Going to be our house. Made of flint. Nestled in a cliff. Looking out to sea.
JOY	It's too late now.
VINCENT	Planned it didn't we? Sat on that god-awful sofa. In our little flat. Night after night. Waiting for Our Carla to be born.

Laughing at the people stuck here forever. The Doreen's and the Maggie's. Their stupid same-everyday-lives. Their gossip. We were going to escape. Make something new. For us and Carla.

JOY   But it didn't work.

VINCENT   Do you remember how we felt?

JOY   *(QUIETLY)* Yes.

VINCENT   Do you remember?

JOY   Yes.

VINCENT   When I was by your side. My skin used to crackle and fizz.

JOY   Mine, mine too.

VINCENT   As soon as I met you. I knew you were the one that I'd nail my flag to the mast for.

JOY   I'd rather have died than not be with you.

VINCENT   Me too.

PAUSE.

JOY   Then you got the job in that place.

VINCENT   We needed money.

JOY   It was only going to be a year.

VINCENT   Eighteen months tops.

JOY   All those years.

VINCENT	The line goes so fast it's hard to keep up.
JOY	Everytime you came home you were further away from me.
VINCENT	I had to forget you each day. To do the job.
JOY	And we're still here in the middle of all…this.
VINCENT	When I got home…you and Carla were so beautiful…and I felt so…
JOY	Why didn't you tell me about the boy?
VINCENT	You wouldn't have understood.
JOY	Why didn't you tell me, Vincent?
VINCENT	I wanted to protect you.
JOY	Why didn't
VINCENT	I tried, but I couldn't bear it!
BEAT.	
VINCENT	I knew you'd hate me. I couldn't bear it if you hated me more than you already do.
JOY	I'm scared.
VINCENT	So am I. I always try to do it properly, Joy. You should understand that.
BEAT.	
JOY	What have you done?

*Enter **ROB**, swigging from a bottle of beer.*

ROB   Alright? Alright?

VINCENT It's laughing boy.

ROB   Nice evening for it, Don't often see stars,
only the dirty orange glow from the city.
Used to look at the stars with me Dad,
we'd...but when I do see stars these days,
sometimes, when I look up and see all
these billions and billions of stars and
other planets and people on these planets
looking at the stars too, when I look up at
the stars I think – fuck 'em, who gives a
shit?

LAUGHS .

            Alright?

Swigs beer.

VINCENT You've had enough.

ROB   I like the nighttime. Loved the dark as a
little kid, I always had, had an affinity
with it. Suits me. The daylight, everyone's
looking at you, trying to work out wh,
what's going on in your head. Why you do
this and that. They think they can rewire

85

you and make you like they want you to be. I don't want to be like that, you know what I want? I want your wallet.

Swigs beer.

VINCENT Go home boy.

ROB Give it me. Once you realise you don't have to be what people want you to be like you can do anything, because what, wha, can anybody do? Your mates can tell you to fuck off. They can laugh at your bruises. Call you chicken. But what can they actually do? People do what they're told cos they're afraid of what will happen if they don't. You smack a kid to stop him being naughty, next time he does what he's told, not because it's right, he does it cos he's scared of what will happen. Simple. Don't fear the smack. Once you know that anything is possible. So give me your wallet.

Swigs beer.

Smashes the bottle. The shard as a weapon in his hand.

ROB You wal, give me your wallet.

VINCENT   Please Rob, stop…

*ROB lunges at **VINCENT**. They fight.*

*ROB tries to stab **VINCENT** with the bottle.*

***VINCENT** beats **ROB** back and **ROB** drops the bottle.*

***VINCENT** picks it up. Holds it out to protect himself.*

VINCENT   That's enough. Enough! You listening?

*ROB rushes forward. **VINCENT'S** arm snaps up and stabs*

ROB in the neck.

ROB falls to the ground. Twitching.

Twitching.

PAUSE.

***VINCENT** kneels by ROB. Inspects the wound on ROB's*

neck.

BEAT.

***VINCENT** picks up the bottle and carefully cuts ROB'S neck*

with it.

And again.

***VINCENT** holds ROB'S hand as the twitching stops.*

***VINCENT** retches for a moment.*

***VINCENT** stands.*

VINCENT	I can tell when something's going to die. Can't be saved. He would have suffered, Joy. Couldn't let that happen.
JOY	Vincent...
VINCENT	Could have been quicker. Should have been quicker. Stuck in a car park. If I'd had the right tools. Would have done it properly. But, but...
JOY	There can be no buts.
VINCENT	See? I knew you'd hate me. What else could I do, Joy?
JOY	There can be no buts, Vincent...because you did the right thing.

JOY takes VINCENT'S hands and examines them.

JOY	I should never have let you stay in that place for so long.
VINCENT	No choice.
JOY	Your hands have so many scars.
VINCENT	Half the time you don't feel the knife cut.
JOY	They're like spaghetti junction.

JOY kisses VINCENT'S hands.

JOY	It can be like it was at the start.

VINCENT   We can leave this place?

JOY   Live in a little house.

VINCENT   By the sea.

JOY   We'll be brand new.

Bone

VINCENT and JOY.

VINCENT My right shoulder fizzes. Must be a nerve. Right on the inside. Fizzes like acid. All those cuts. Wakes me up at night. Joy thinks I should see a Doctor. No point. They'd tell me to rest. To stop. No need. Won't matter soon. Need to hang on.

Feel queasy all day. On the job. The stench. Not noticed it for years. Now it's all I can do to keep my lunch in. Invades me. Makes my bones ache.

Struggle to keep up with the line. Got a warning from the shift manager. Other day. Not working fast enough. Threatens to cut my pay. Never missed a shift. Never been on the sick. Seventeen years and they give me a warning. Jumped up little...I do the job. Stay quiet. Wait all day. So I can get home to Joy. So I can smell her. Feel her. She makes the sickness pass. Until the next day. I wait all day. So I can get home to Joy. Can't do it much longer. Too fast for me. Can't keep up. Have to hang in there. For Joy. A little longer. Only a little longer.

JOY   Four more days.

VINCENT   I know.

JOY   Four more days and we will have you out of there.

VINCENT   I can do it.

JOY   I know you can.

VINCENT   All I want is for us to be together.

JOY   We will be, we already are.

VINCENT   Away from all of this.

JOY   Everything starts again.

VINCENT   I can do this.

JOY   Four days.

VINCENT   Only four days.

JOY   I've nearly packed everything, and the van's booked for ten am Saturday.

VINCENT   We could leave everything. Go now.

JOY   Four days and we will leave here.

VINCENT   Never come back.

JOY   I promise you.

VINCENT	Good.
JOY	To the sea.
VINCENT	Fresh air.
JOY	Fresher than any air we've ever breathed.
VINCENT	And the sea?
JOY	Will wash everything away.
VINCENT	For us.
JOY	For us. I unhooked the phone. It kept ringing and ringing, Doreen or Maggie. I haven't told them we're going, especially after Maggie's Roy. That Doreen, at death's door she said Roy was, weeks to live she said, cancer she said – irritable bowel syndrome apparently. Maggie's livid, she won't get her new wallpaper...(LAUGHS)... I don't care. But Mr Patel was so upset when I quit word, will have gone round, they'll know.
VINCENT	Patel...
JOY	He's been good, Vincent, he's paid me up until the end of the month, and there's still two weeks to go.

BEAT.

JOY	What we're doing is right, isn't it?
VINCENT	You want to. Don't you?
JOY	It's...Chrissy.
VINCENT	They'll have to let him go. Have to.
JOY	I know. It's just...
VINCENT	I know.
JOY	But if we told them, they'd...
VINCENT	Yes. You still want to go?
JOY	More than anything.
VINCENT	Then it's right.
JOY	I have my Vincent back.
VINCENT	Then we go.

Enter CARLA

CARLA	I cannot believe you're going.
JOY	You've had three weeks to get used to it.
CARLA	Three weeks to get my head round your midlife crisis.
JOY	This was always the plan.
CARLA	Where do I live?
VINCENT	You can stay here.
JOY	Until it sells.
CARLA	How long will that take?

JOY	Hopefully not long.
CARLA	No one's going to want to buy a house round here.
VINCENT	On cheap.
JOY	The agent thinks someone'll snap it up to rent, people like that are always on the lookout for a bargain.
CARLA	Then where do I live?
JOY	You could come with us.
CARLA	I told you, I'm staying.
VINCENT	Come with us.
CARLA	Everything I know is here, I won't run away from this town.
VINCENT	There's nothing left.
CARLA	This is where we live.
JOY	If you want to stay, then stay, but we have to go.
CARLA	I won't have enough cash on my own.
JOY	You could ask work for more hours.
CARLA	Pub's barely busy enough to keep it open on a Saturday. They're not gonna give me more work.
VINCENT	We'll send you what we can, but-

CARLA	-you can't go. This place, it needs our help, things won't get better if people leave.
VINCENT	Nothing we can do.
JOY	Carla, love
CARLA	You can't just go.
JOY	It's now or never. We've found this lovely little place to rent until the house sells.
VINCENT	Looks out to the sea.
JOY	It's small, but it looks beautiful, I'll get a job in local shop, shouldn't be too hard, your Dad…
VINCENT	I'll find something.
JOY	It's exciting isn't it?
CARLA	This town needs us.
JOY	No one will notice we've gone.
CARLA	Sandra needs us.
JOY	Sandra's fine.
CARLA	No she's not.
VINCENT	Can't change anything.
JOY	Sandra will be alright.
CARLA	She tried to top herself last night.
BEAT.	
JOY	*(QUIETLY)* Oh Sandra.

VINCENT   Will she live?

CARLA   In hospital, but she's alive. I thought that gossip hotline would have been ringing off the hook.

JOY   I don't talk to...not anymore.

CARLA   This is all Hinton's fault. It's going to trial and he's still saying he didn't do it.

JOY   Poor Sandra.

VINCENT   Should we stay?

CARLA   He's making it worse for her, she just wants to know what happened.

JOY   No, no we have to go, there's nothing we can do.

CARLA   She needs us all here to help her.

VINCENT   Nothing we can do.

CARLA   She's your friend.

JOY   We've made our choices.

CARLA   This town is crumbling down. You can see it in the people, they look brittle. The things we did a couple of weeks ago felt so right, but now...and nothing's changed. No one knows what to do anymore. I'm afraid. I'm afraid the town's breaking up and we can't stop it.

VINCENT   If it's dead then best let it be dead.

CARLA   I had this fear when I was a kid that one of you would die. If I thought about it I'd get the shakes, like the ones you get after a massive night out. If anyone ever hurt either of you, I'd go nuts. Berserk. I'd kill them. No messing. I could kill My, I could kill Mark and Kylie Philips right now, but it's not the same as someone hurting you.

BEAT.

There are times when I could kill both of you, loads of times. Everyday. Sometimes I think there's no way we're related. Look at you, neither of you has any dress sense, but you're my Mum and Dad. I couldn't handle it if you got hurt, I just couldn't take it. Like Sandra can't take it.

If Hinton had any heart in him he'd tell Sandra what happened and stop her suffering.

PAUSE.

JOY	You're a good girl, Carla.
CARLA	I spent all the memorial money on flowers. I didn't know what else to do.
JOY	She's a good girl, Vincent.
CARLA	They're being sent to the hospital tomorrow. I just need to write a card to go with them, but I don't know what to say.
VINCENT	She always has been.
CARLA	Crazy flowers with a million different colours to wake Sandra up and make her feel alive again.
VINCENT	That's how we brought you up - our daughter.
JOY	You were a beautiful baby too.
VINCENT	We looked after you.
JOY	You were, such a bonny thing.
CARLA	A right snooty cow in the florists.
VINCENT	Made sure you can stand up for yourself.
JOY	I know you're biased about your own
CARLA	She starts giving me all this attitude just because I don't know what types of flowers to get.

JOY	but I was so pleased, because some babies when they're born they look
VINCENT	Taught you right from wrong.
JOY	they have funny shaped heads
CARLA	So I gave her, "I don't want any trouble, lady, cos I'm feeling a bit tense. I just want the flowers."
JOY	and they're all blotchy aren't they?
CARLA	Starts giving it all about different flowers mean different things.
JOY	I never like the look of other people's babies
CARLA	Roses for love, lilies for death.
JOY	but Carla, the second I saw you, a dear little thing, your eyes all scrunched up
VINCENT	Your Mum fought so hard to make sure you were safe.
JOY	I thought you were the most beautiful thing I had ever seen.
VINCENT	Fought like a lioness. But something's not right. Alarms. Midwifes rush to the monitors. The baby is under stress. Your

	heartbeat's dropping. They had to cut your Mum open.
JOY	All I cared about was keeping you alive.
CARLA	"Say it with Flowers" the shop's called. Snooty cow asks what I want?
VINCENT	They bring in this young lad. To do the cutting. He's no older than some of the lads sweeping up the abattoir. Doctors should be middle aged.
CARLA	I give her my best 'Do *not* mess with me' look and say' "You can stop that bollocks right now."
VINCENT	He's got skill. This Dr Pimples. Precision. I'll give him that.
JOY	Felt like someone doing the washing up in my stomach.
VINCENT	I watch his eyes above his mask. Never flicker. Never look away.
JOY	I wondered what I looked like, opened up to the world.
VINCENT	I was shocked by how the inside of you looked so different to the sheep and the pigs.

JOY	What they'd find in there.
VINCENT	It shouldn't have. All the parts are the same. But it takes my breath away.
CARLA	Her Royal Stuckupiness is not happy with the way I talk to her. She's going to call the cops. Tell my parents.
VINCENT	It doesn't bother the doctor.
JOY	And they found you.
VINCENT	All in day's work to him.
CARLA	Suddenly the flower fairy goes all quiet. I like to think it was cos of my engrossing personality, but it was probably the bread bag of cash that I chucked on the counter.
VINCENT	He's done thousands.
JOY	I knew you looked like your Dad.
VINCENT	Just another on the line.
JOY	Knew it before I even saw you.
VINCENT	They lift my daughter out. I cut the cord. They take you to be weighed. Measured. Checked. Do you get the all clear?
CARLA	Suddenly she loves me, running around picking out all these flowers for me.
JOY	And when I did see you

VINCENT	They give you to me.
JOY	your Dad holding you.
CARLA	I want Sandra to be surrounded by all these colours.
VINCENT	I'm looking down at this little creature.
CARLA	Red and yellow and green and blue.
JOY	I knew then
VINCENT	I felt then
JOY	That we were more
VINCENT	than just love.
JOY	You made us
VINCENT	blood
JOY	skin
VINCENT	and bone.
CARLA	I have all these flowers, but I don't know what to say to Sandra on this stupid little card.
JOY	And we swore then
VINCENT	in front of all the doctors and nurses
JOY	that we'd always do the right thing by you.
VINCENT	And for you.

JOY	What would we be if we broke that promise?

*Enter **ROB** who stands next to the family.*

CARLA	What do you think I should say?
VINCENT	Tell her.
JOY	Tell her that we're sorry. That your Dad had no choice.
CARLA	What kind of message is that?
VINCENT	Tell Sandra that I killed her boy.

Moment.

The deafening sound of the abattoir at work — cattle being brought in, machinery.

The sounds fade.

END.